Letters to my Life

AK DEBOER

Letters To My Life
By AK deBoer

Editing by Kristy deBoer
Formatting and cover design by Erica Alexander at Serendipity Formats.

Contents

Playlist

1. **Somewhere in Neverland** – All Time Low
2. **Walk on Water or Drown** – Mayday Parade
3. **Sympathy** – Goo Goo Dolls
4. **Not Standing Alone** – Alexz Johnson
5. **I Hope You Dance** – Lee Ann Womack
6. **Kinda Over It** – Young Culture
7. **Chicago Is So Two Years Age** – Fall Out Boy
8. **Who I Am Hates Who I've Been** – Relient K
9. **From The Outside** – Real Friends
10. **I'm Just a Kid** – Simple Plan
11. **Ready To Fall** – Rise Against
12. **Closing Time** – Semisonic
13. **Swing Life Away** – Rise Against

Little Ways

"This song made me think of you."
"Do you want to get together soon?"
"Are you home yet?"
"Have you eaten?"
"Please be safe."
"I miss you."
"I'm proud of you."
"I wish you were home."
"You make me feel safe."
"You were my first call."
"Can I put you as my emergency contact?"
"I got this for you."
"You should read this."
"I prayed for you."
"Text me when you get home."
"Do you want anything?"
"Thanks for telling me."
I love you.

Neverland

I used to want so desperately to be normal
Now I want to be anything but
A normal life is great
Until I land a job I hate
And all my friends move away
And I have to smile through the pain
And every day's the same
It's everything I ever wanted
I followed my dreams, right?
But not really
Because when a voice cried out begging me to leave
I stomped it down
I believed a job was just a job
And it can be
And I'd be happy
Then I heard this voice in the back of my head
And she said
"Remember when you used to write poetry?
Remember me?"

Of course I did
But I buried her so deep
I didn't think she'd ever get out
Covered her in dirt and called it reality
But when the earth shook
She crawled her way out
And reminded me of when I used to dream
And everything wasn't about money
She claims it still doesn't have to be
I want so desperately to believe.

Mayday

The world's not bad, it's just broken
Can we take just this moment
Let's make this better

For the kids of tomorrow
And the kids of today
For the kids we never got the chance to be

Cause we were busy picking up debris
The rubble from the riots and the pieces of our sanity
And the stress to be perfect
An expectation we could never meet
But we'd die trying
Or spend the night crying

For the kids of tomorrow
And the kids of today
For the kids we never got the chance to be

Cause the world stole our innocence
And told us we weren't good enough
Said we were lazy and whiney and sensitive and -----
HYPOCRITES!
But the fact is we were broken by the world they made
And left terrified we couldn't undo all their mistakes

For the kids of tomorrow
And the kids of today
For the kids we hope they get the chance to be.

Pyromaniac

I've been burning bridges my whole life
I claim it's for protection
That it's just how I survive
Or maybe I just like fire
There's something so comforting
About knowing I can't go back
Until I get lonely
Remembering how you used to hold me
I pull out my phone
Go to the number I should have deleted long ago
Not that I could forget it if I tried
Not that I've actually tried
I almost click call for the umpteenth time
But I turn it off
Turn my TV up
Drown out thoughts of you
Til I get through
Because the fire has long since died

And I'm left cold
And alone
Surrounded by ashes of who I used to call home.

Concerts

I want a man who will go to concerts with me
I think that will tell me all I need to know
Will he dance and scream even though he doesn't know the
words
Or will he sit in the corner and make the whole night worse
Because I need a man who will have a good time just because
I am
Because he gets to hold me in his arms and see me smile
Not someone who will make me feel guilty for having fun
Will he put himself between me and the pit
Put me in front of him so I can see
Will he line up for doors with me
Even when it feels like negative ten degrees
I want a man who will go to concerts with me
I think that's really all I need

The Past is Alive and Well

I loved you a lot
But at first only a little
And at some point not at all
I saw some good things in you
I made up the rest
Just to pretend that I knew you
Then I did know you
And the real you was better
So much better than I'd hoped
I say loved, past tense
To pretend that I've let go
But the truth is it's present tense
And I fear it might always be so
I think a part of me will always love you
I hope you feel that way too
You healed me in ways I didn't expect
Of course you broke me like that too
But in case you ever question it
I have long since forgiven you.

Fine Line

I have to spend the rest of my life with you.
And I hate it
I hate the way you look
And the way you talk and act
And I hate myself for hating you
Because I know I'm not supposed to
Because you've been there through all my ups and downs
And made sure when I fell,
I never stayed too long on the ground
And when I look in the mirror
I want to love what I see
I'm working on it, I promise
But it's hard to love what you once hated
Hard to realize that our love is fated
When I look in the mirror
I see someone who gets up every day and tries
Even on those days when she'd rather just cry
And I'm starting to talk to her like someone I love

Because I know after all that she's done
She deserves someone who says
I get to spend the rest of my life with you.

Hating you is like holding a knife to my
hand and hoping you'll bleed, and
sometimes, I think it's worth it

I picture him like a child
I mean he's still grown
But like a child in the corner
Sad and alone
You ask if I would hurt him?
If I could?
But he's done more to himself than I ever would
I wish him the best
I really do
There's an ache in my chest for all he's been through
Not that he didn't put me through it too
I can't let him back into my life
He'll only hurt me again
But it must be a real hard existence
Having no friends
I've forgiven him
A long time ago now
Even if some people don't understand how
They claim to forgive you have to reconcile

In response I only smile
Because while I haven't reconciled with him
I've reconciled with the truth
That it was never about me
I've moved on and found peace
I hope the same for him.

How Do I Tell You?

If you called right now,
I'd answer the phone
Because I still remember when we were girls
Trying to figure out how to save the world
I think we both got lost somewhere along the way
And when we found ourselves again
We didn't make sense
I wanted what was best for you then
I still want what's best for you now
But you couldn't see that
I don't think you tried
And that's not the accusation it sounds like
Because I didn't try either
Somewhere along the way
I think we both realized
All we could do was save ourselves
We forgot about the world
Just tried to escape our own personal hells
I really hope you did

That you got everything you wanted
And I hope you know
If you called right now,
I'd still answer the phone
I think we'd still feel like home.

Eulogy

I'm not mourning you now
You're not worth it
I'm mourning who you were
Because that was someone different
Who you are now
Is someone I am happy to lose
But I will always grieve the person you used to be
You say I'm crazy
Claim you haven't changed
But I guarantee
The person I see now and the person I saw then
Are not the same
Maybe that's on me
I saw the good in you
But now it's all tainted
Where I used to paint you in vivid color
I can only see shades of grey
That's perfectly okay
Really it's not your fault

People change, people grow
I didn't like who you grew into
And you felt the same about me
Sometimes love dies
I can let us rest in peace

All I Wanted

Is it wrong to not want anyone to know
But want to be known nonetheless?
Because I don't want to share my secrets
I don't want to bare my soul
But I want seeing you to feel like coming home.
I want you to see me, but I won't tear down my wall
I want you to know me, but I can't get past it
I talk in abstracts because concrete scares me
And I write it down because I don't want to talk at all
So, this is my apology
To everyone I've ever loved
Who I never gave the chance to love me.

To My Niece

I hope you stay innocent
But I am tarnished
I hope you stay innocent
But I was dealt a different hand
I hope you never understand
I hope the world always looks like sunshine
And the grass always smells like rain
I hope you never know this pain
And though I know I can't stop it
I at least want to try
I wish boys never broke hearts
And girls never cried
But they do
And I hope that's the worst pain you go through
I hope there's always a next big adventure
And your dreams are so big you get called crazy
I hope you die having lived a life without fear
And I hope you know I'll always be here

Pillow Talk

I said scream
Take it out on me
Let me help you breathe
Pull you from beneath
Save you from yourself
You are safe with me
I'll hold you while you bleed
Rest your head on me
I'll wait here while you sleep
Help you find your peace
Go ahead and scream

The Boy I Made Up

I dreamt about you again last night
I don't know why
I know you're out of my league
I know you'd rather be with her than me
I don't blame you
Please don't think I do
I'm not even hurt
Because objectively I see the truth
But I dreamt about you again tonight
I keep thinking it should be us
In another life I think it is
I think you'd make me feel safe
Let me take up space
And I don't really know you
Not like I do in my head
But I keep dreaming about you
It's hard not to
I mean look at you
You're cute and you're kind and you always know the time

It sounds stupid when I say it like that
But I keep dreaming about you
I wish I didn't know why
I think then it'd be easier to stop
Because I shouldn't be dreaming about you
But you go to church more than I do
I really like that about you
I could list all the reasons
But I won't waste my words
Knowing that even though you're not hers
You'll probably never be mine
But I still dream about you all the time
It's more when I'm awake than when I'm asleep
Pretending one day you'll dream about me.

Point of View

I wonder how it ended in your head
Did you vilify me to all our old friends?
Because I let go, that's a choice I made
But I let go without justifying my escape
So, they probably all see me
As the bitch who stopped responding
But nobody asked me
Why I stopped trying
I wasn't worth their wasted breath
It's as simple as that
I'm not even sure I would have told them the truth if they'd
asked
And all's well that ends well
And it would have ended just the same
Because I got sick and tired of playing your game
You know she used to shit talk you to all her friends
But it looks like you did a fine job of getting rid of them
I wonder if she knows now what I knew then

That you only care about yourself in the end
And maybe I'm wrong
Was I just not worth your time?
Because you seem to have plenty of lifelong friends
So, I wonder why you weren't mine.

Sunsets

I want sunsets with you
And I know how it sounds
An overplayed cliche
But it's not about the sun
Or the beauty
And I'm sorry to say
It's not about you
It's about having spent the day together
And watching the sun go down
Knowing that we'll spend the night together too
It's about my favorite time of day
Watching the sky turn colors that never fail to make me smile
It's about sharing it with someone
And I want that someone to be you
And if in time, I want sunsets with someone else
I hope the sunsets will still make me think of you
When I watched the sky
And you watched me
When you kissed me as the sky turned pink

When you held me as darkness finally overtook the light
When you told me I was more beautiful than the whole night
And I called you a liar
And you just held me tighter
I think I'll always want sunsets with you
Would you want that, too?

608

A warm May breeze blows
The path ahead is long
As the flight lifts into the air
And we head toward the light of the sun
There's a deep sense of sorrow
For what we leave behind
The halls and stairwells
That room, now just a beginning
It's a strange window of time
Throughout these months, it became a home
And we became a family
The scents of candles and perfumes and dining hall foods
Now a faint memory that we hope to never lose.

My Oldest Friend

I still keep our picture on my wall
We were young then
I would have sworn we had it all
Didn't know yet what was to unfold
The secrets they kept hidden in the walls
There's a piece of me still stuck in that place
That couldn't grow up
So I kept her safe
I'm sorry I couldn't do the same for you
I should have tried harder
But we were just kids
I should have tried harder
I'm sorry that I didn't
You deserved better
Than what you got
You still deserve better
You deserve whatever you want
You were pure

And they left you damaged
I'm sorry I couldn't change the cards you were handed

Standing Alone

I can see her dancing by herself
Not waiting for a man to join her
Though she wouldn't shoo him away if he did
The music's loud
Drowning out the talk of the crowd
They can say what they want about her
But she'll keep dancing on her own
Because she promised her mom that she would
It's all she ever asked
Was that given the chance
She would dance

Too Young

I'm 19 and in debt
Filled with regret
Not knowing what to do next
Because I might be psyching myself out
But I don't know how
I can do this now
They lied to me
Oh the hypocrisy
Because I'm not as good at this as I was told
Why do they let us make decisions at 18 years old?

2024

Why are our politicians preaching hate
Don't they see it's not okay
My neighbor hates me
Because we don't share the same beliefs
I don't blame them
Because it's what they've been fed
By all these politicians
Out for each other's heads
Never speaking of what they've done right
Only what someone else has done wrong
When did empathy go out the window?
When did the why stop counting?
Because you don't care for my explanation
Your politics became your religion
And you have made it your mission
To eradicate people who don't think the same
So, before you sit there and judge
Try to lead with love
It'll cause you a lot less pain.

Generational Trauma

The women that came before me scream
They bicker and fight
Hold onto grudges with all their might
I didn't hear the screams
But I felt the echo
Felt the emptiness of never knowing
Who I could have loved
Who they pushed away
Saw the void that was left
Saw the hurt in their eyes
That they tried so desperately to hide
I watched the next generation try to heal the wounds
Left by matriarchs who only wanted love
Who never felt enough
They chose anger over pain
But anger's the damnedest thing
Because it continues burning you
Even as you snatch your hand back from the flame
They played their parts

Pretending they felt nothing
But we all saw the holes that were left
The silence somehow louder than the screams
As we try to heal the wounds
Left by the matriarchs
Of our broken family

I'm Kinda Over It

Everything I thought I'd never get over, I did
Which is why I know, I'll get over you
You won't be easy
It'll take time
But at some point, your residence will move to the back of
my mind
Slipping further and further away from my consciousness
Until it will seem I have forgotten you all together
Maybe I'll make decisions differently because I knew you
In fact, I'm certain I will
But for all intents and purposes, you'll be forgotten
I will get over you
Someday our song will come on and I'll smile thinking about
how you used to sing it with so much passion
You'll force your way to the front of my mind for that moment
But then, the song will end
And my day will continue
I might think *man I miss you*

But then you'll slip right back to your house in my
subconscious
Leaving the door unlatched for the next time I call you out
But I won't think of you again for a really long time
I will get over you
I always do

The Aftermath

Someday there's gonna be a version of me
That you don't know
I would love to believe that
But I don't
Not because you get to see it all through a phone
But you do
Because I never bothered blocking you
There is no before and after you
Parts of me will always echo parts of you
Because I loved you once
I looked at you and saw things I liked
I absorbed those things to be more like you
Because I liked you once
I don't now.
I'm not even sure I understand why I ever did
I don't see those things in you now
That I liked back then
You shed those parts of yourself

But I know they're in me
So there will never be a version of me that you don't know
Because part of me is part of you
Even if I am not part of you now

Chicago

I tell you I think Chicago's the greatest city in the world
And you tell me you've never been
So, I waste my time trying to describe it to you
Knowing damn well I can't capture it in words
I tell you about the river
That's so beautiful aquamarine
And sometimes it's green
And once it was Cubby blue
I tell you about being a Bears fan and a Cubs fan
About being always so close but so far
But believing it anyway with your whole heart
And about riding the pink line into Douglas Park
Because Riot Fest in the rain feels like home
And about real Chicago pizza
Tavern style not deep dish
And I tell you about The Pier and Buckingham Fountain
And you tell me it sounds nice
And I swear one day I'll show you it's magical

And you'll see the skyline that never fails to take my breath away
And you'll agree Chicago's the best city in the world

The Secrets I Keep

You don't get to know I cried so hard I puked last night
Cause you decided you were sick of being in my life
You don't get to know that I still pray for you sometimes
That I really hope all your plans turn out just right
I hope you get your perfect little life
Without me
Hope you finally reconcile with your family
You're not my problem anymore
I let go a while ago
So I hope you're good and you're happy
Hope you're living just fine without me
But I don't need to know.

Handprints

I still feel your handprints on me
It's in everything I do
It's in the way I speak
Even though I know
I had to let you go
I still feel your handprints on me
And it's not physical
But the way I move
Is different because of you
Something forever altered in my brain
I don't think I'll ever be the same
I still feel your handprints on me
Like a child leaves them
In wet cement
Innocent but permanent
Forever changed
Even if we didn't know then
I still feel your handprints on me

And strange enough
It helps me sleep

Good Company

You, my dear, are always good company
Even when you're crying on the bathroom floor
Because your relationship just doesn't work anymore
I'll still be next to you
Even when I have to hold your hair back while you puke
And hold your hand all night
Make you dance to forget
Please don't apologize
For all the times he makes you cry
Because I know where your heart is
And he doesn't treat it right
But even if you choose him for the rest of your life
I will stay by your side
Because even on your worst nights
You, my dear, are always good company.

Who I've Been Hates Who I Am

I miss you
But not as much as I miss the person I was when I was with you
I'm trying not to spend forever mourning the past
But lately all I can do is that
Because I'm not the same as I was before
In some ways I'm better
And in some ways, I'm worse
I guess that's just how life works
But I still miss that girl
That believed in everything
In the goodness of people
And believed in love and second chances
I still believe in those things
But I'm jaded now
I believe people are good but most show me they're not
I believe in love but not that someone will love me
I believe people can change but I'm scared to stick around to
find out
I like myself but I can't see why anyone else would.

Healing

I no longer hate the things you once loved
I did
For a while there I did
I thought I always would
And it terrified me
That you still had that power
Even though we'd cut ties long ago
I loved those things once too
But for a while I could only think of you
I still do
But it's not overwhelming like it was
It's not ripping my heart from my chest again
Missing who used to be my best friend
It's an ache more than a pain
If that makes any sense
It barely hurts when I hear that song
But I still hear your voice when I sing along
I buy your favorite candies and enjoy them by myself

And it's all okay
I still miss you
Just in a different way

The man Who Left

I'm afraid
Afraid that one day they'll ask about you
And I won't know what to say
And even more afraid that I will
Afraid that I won't see you again
And even more afraid that I will
Afraid that you'll die alone
Afraid that I'll be forced to go to your funeral
Afraid they'll ask me to speak
And I won't know what to say again
Even more afraid that I will
And they'll hate me for saying it
Not because I won't mean it
I will.
Not because they won't believe it
They know.
Not because you don't deserve it
You do.

But it's wrong to speak ill of the dead
And it's wrong to breathe a sigh of relief
Then again, I deserve to feel safe too
And I'm finally safe from you.

A Limerick for Bacon

I never said thank you for all you've done for me
The truth is we've never been that sap-py
Even when we fight
I still root for you with all my might
You have always been the best of our family tree

From the Outside

I'm a listener at heart
Someone who sits on the side of the room and observes
Picking up breadcrumbs as they're heard
Piecing together what I can
But never knowing the full story
I was not born this way
I was made
I had no choice
With everyone I let in, leaving me more broken
I can't help but keep people at arm's length
Not pushing them away
But not pulling them in either
I'm always there but no one talks to me
Not really
Not when it matters
They'll tell me about their day
But not about their real life
Maybe I'm self-absorbed to think it's about me

But what else am I supposed to think
So, I sit on the edge of the room
Watching and listening
Too afraid of being overbearing
But silently begging them to tell me everything

Friendsgiving

You invited me to Friendsgiving this year
In the old group chat that's been dormant all summer
I assumed you had created another
Without me
I didn't blame you because I would have too
But you sent the text in the old group chat
And not for the first time, I wondered
What stories you'd been told
Or if I came up at all
I assumed you hadn't thought about me since last fall
I sat on my couch and contemplated going
Because a part of me still misses you all
But I know that part's been gone for a while
I'm not the girl I was in high school
I don't miss you now
I miss you then
And if I went now, I'd no longer fit in
You'd look at me with confusion
Wondering where I'd gone

That's if you even looked at me
I know as soon as I left
You'd start talking shit
Not that I'd blame you, that's not it
But why show up when I know you don't want me there
You can talk shit the whole night and I don't have to care
Yet still when the time came
I thought about grabbing my keys
Feeling like I still owed some of you a part of me
Tell me... when they start saying things
Will you defend me
When they start telling stories
Will you say that doesn't sound right
Or will you let them drag me through the mud
I won't blame you either way
Just curious
What you'd say?

Favorite

I'm nobody's favorite
I'm not sure that I ever have been
And usually, I'm okay with that
Not happy, but resigned
And then other times
It feels like my heart's being ripped from my chest
And I want to scream and cry
About how it's unfair
And that I don't understand why
But who would I cry to?
Because I'm nobody's favorite
And if I say that to anyone
They'll lie to placate me
I don't have a favorite they'll say
And maybe that's true
But if they did,
I know it wouldn't be me
Because I am nobody's favorite
And why would I be?

Choices

"I don't wanna die," she said
"You don't wanna live," I responded
I think that sums up the two types of people in this world
Because you can either be afraid to die
Or afraid to only ever survive
And I think I'll always be more afraid to merely survive
I'd jump off a cliff with you if you asked
I believe more yeses than nos leads you down the best path
Maybe this life isn't for everyone
Maybe it's not stories that feed your soul
But for me it is
For me it's the only way I can live
Because I don't fear death
I fear dying never having had a life

The Ferd

I don't want to leave
I'm not done here yet
I'm gonna miss all of them
We made a home on these floors
And now I may never see them again
I mean of course I will
But that's besides the point
Because I'll never see them like this again
They won't be my neighbors
Our friendship will be active instead of passive
Or it'll be nothing at all
Please don't let it be nothing at all.

All Because I Was Just a Kid

Sometimes I wonder who I'd be today
If I knew then what I know now
Maybe my life would be forever changed
But honestly I don't know how
I think I'd make the same mistakes
Believe the wrong people
Wrong the right people
Try it anyway because I'm stubborn
Forgive too much
Regret too little
Recklessly choose who to love
Because the heart does what it does
I think I'd be fine with my life repeating
Just as it has, however fleeting
Given a chance to do it all over
I think I'd do it just the same
The good was worth the pain.

The Lie

You forget that not everyone grew up like you did
It's always there
Of course, it's always there
But the cracks become so small
You can pretend they aren't there
Almost like you've been repaired

But then, sometimes it slaps you in the face
It hits you like a physical ache
It brings tears to your eyes
For no reason
Because you've healed, right?
Or maybe that's a lie

A lie you tell yourself
You want it to be true
You almost believe it too
Almost, but you don't
Not really

You don't know what you're missing
But sometimes you do

It exists in you, of course
But it's just a part of you
It's not who you are
It doesn't control your actions
Not why you push people away
Even when they beg you to stay
You are so healed from it
You talk as if it isn't you

Or maybe that's me.
It resides in me
Sometimes like a ditch
But sometimes like a crater
Most of the time I forget
But sometimes I can't.

I Was Only a Child

You will never meet my kids
I decided that in 5th grade
I was 10.
You won't be at my wedding
I decided that in 6th grade
I was 11.
You won't be at my graduation
I decided that in 8th grade
I was 13.
You won't know anything about my life
I decided that in 10th grade
I was 15.
I couldn't drive
But I made that decision
I knew I had to get out
It doesn't seem to eat at you
The way it does me
The cigarettes burned in my memory
Just like they burned my arm all those years ago

A phantom scar I swear I can still see
I can forgive
But apparently, I can't let go
Some days I swear it will swallow me whole
Keeps me trapped
Won't let me let anyone in
It's scary the way it sticks in my skin
I still live with the effects of your sins

Abroad

I know I can do it
Because I watched you do it first
Terrified as you were
You packed your bags and boarded a plane
Left behind everything
And the things you left
They stayed unchanged
Anxiously awaiting your return
Anxious as I am
I watched you do it first

Ready to Fall

I think I might die alone.
I say that with a smile and a shrug
And people give me an awkward laugh
Because they think it's a joke
And mostly it is

I'm pretty sure I'm going to die alone.
Not really
Not completely at least
But without being in love
Loved but not in love
No one to go home to
No one to hold at night
No one that feels like light

I'll probably die alone.
And I'm not really sure why that is
Because I try to be a good person
I think I'd make a good wife

I'm not ugly, not gorgeous, just okay

I don't want to die alone.
I scream from rooftops in my mind
A silent cry for help
That's met with a chuckle
As I die a little inside

Our Moment

I'm waiting for you
Impatiently, but waiting nonetheless
Terrified you'll never find me
But knowing that you're out there
You have to be
Constantly wondering if I've already met you
Worried that I was meant to
But that we missed our moment
But when it's meant to be
You can't miss your moment
That's what I keep reminding myself
I have to
Because I know that true love exists
And I could never forgive myself
If I didn't wait for it

Every New Beginning

Nothing hurts more than knowing it'll end
Because when it does end
The next thing comes along
Life keeps going
You almost get too distracted to realize that it ended
Only you know something is missing
But your life has changed so much
You figure out how to continue
Hold on to people you need to
Let go of the people you can
Because even if you don't want to,
There are people you *can* let go of
It will hurt
But your bandwidth isn't infinite
So you learn to hold on
And let go
Knowing that both those things are hard
But worth it in the end

But knowing it'll end?
Knowing one day you won't live down the hall
Or even in the same city
That hours-long drives layout between us
We'll miss birthdays and babies
Your kids probably won't call me auntie
I won't be able to text you to get lunch on a random Tuesday
They'll be something beautiful in the next phase
I'm not worried about that
Because we'll plan trips
You'll tell your kids we're coming next week
And they'll get excited
They get to see their best friends
That they only get to see twice a year
And we do too
The next part will be great
Of that I'm sure
But this part will end first
And knowing that?
I'm convinced nothing hurts worse.

One Day

Someone is gonna love you so much one day
I love you now but it's not the same
I see your soul and don't know who's to blame
That you haven't been loved like you should
That he takes your heart
And tears you apart
And doesn't appreciate all your good.
But someone is gonna love you so much one day
Because I see your soul
I know it's pure gold
And one day someone will buy you flowers just because
And remember your favorite ice cream
Trust you beyond words and buy you a ring that feels just right
That someone is gonna love you so much one day
I can't wait to wipe my tears
As you say I do
Because someone is gonna love you so much one day
It's impossible not to.

There's Still Time

I haven't fallen in love yet
But I think I want to
I want to have someone to come home to
To call when life gets really good or really bad
I want to have someone to build a life with
Then again, I like the life I'm building on my own
And I think my mom might always be my first call
I don't mind that right now
This life is only mine
I haven't fallen in love yet
And I'm not sure I want to
At least not yet
I'm still busy falling in love with me.

Midwest Boy

He grew up two towns over
I let a Midwest boy steal my heart
Culver's over In-N-Out and no road trips too far
Never started drinking
Too afraid of being like his dad
Ten years sober next November
But my Midwest boy, he still remembers
Swears he'll never be like that
Though by the power of God, he's forgiven his dad
I don't know that I have
Because this boy deserved so much better than that
We go to church before Sunday supper
Switching off weeks whose family gets to host
He feels like home
He makes me feel safe, in a way I'm not sure I ever have
The kind of safe that I thought was reserved for the girls who
grew up behind picket fences
He calls it "our" garden even though he takes care of it

He holds me on the couch watching a movie he doesn't care
about
Comes home with groceries we needed but I didn't ask him
to buy
Because he's a grown up
He learned to braid hair
Said when we have a daughter he would need to know
Makes my favorite dinners on my bad days
And thanks to him I feel okay
I could never give him as much as he gives me
But I try anyway
And he says "You're enough just by being you."
Really its more corny than sweet
Yet here I sit kicking my feet
This is love
It's all it ever was
Two people trying to make each other's lives a little better
Because when you love someone,
That's all you want to do
And if you're really lucky, like me,
That's all they want too

Mom

I've never written a poem for you
Because every poem I've ever written has been about you
The underlying theme is
I made it through
And every time, it was thanks to you
You are in between the lines of everything I have ever written
I didn't want to be sentimental about it
But I wanted to make sure you knew
Why I've never written a poem for you
The truth is every time I choose to continue
I hear your voice in the back of my head urging me on
You are my safe place and my first call
It is because of you that I can write
That I can get past it
And write it down
And process it
And try
Every poem I've ever written has been for you
Because I could never write just one for you

Burnt Toast

I almost cried
Because I burnt my toast this morning
Except it wasn't just the burnt toast
But it was the last straw
I missed my alarm
My shower was cold
My phone was nearly dead
And then I burnt my toast
So, I took an extra 5 minutes to make new toast

I missed my usual train
Because I burnt my toast
So I got on a different train
Which took me to a different station
Which took me on a different walk
And I bumped into a man who was holding coffee
And his coffee spilled all down his shirt
And I had to stop to apologize

Even though I was late for work
Because I burnt my toast
And he and I talked for longer than we should have
Because we were both already late
And I couldn't stop looking at his eyes
Or his smile
Or his heart

I think I met my soul mate
Because this morning I burnt my toast.

Walnut Street

There's a porch that's seen it all
Every new baby brought home for the first time
Every late night goodbye
Every hardship that made us feel lost
There's a porch that's welcomed us with open arms
That in the dead of winter still feels warm
When I picture home, I picture that porch
And I imagine I'm not the only one
Who breathes a little easier when it comes into view
And I know it's not the porch
It's the people that feel like home
The safety net that's always there
I hope I have a porch like that one day
That I make a porch like that
That years from now my grandkids will say
Can we sit on the porch?
I'll wave goodbye to them as they leave
Standing on a porch of my own

I'll think of the first porch that felt like home
And I'll sit on my porch
Writing letters to my life.

About the Author

AK deBoer is a college student studying civil engineering and creative writing. She started writing poetry when she was very young but took a long hiatus before resuming in college. In her free time, she loves attending concerts (especially pop-punk, emo, and nu-metal) and spending time with family and friends. She also loves romance books, good burgers, and traveling. She has released her debut poetry book Letters to my Life and is currently working on her next poetry book and a YA novel.

Connect with AK deBoer at:
Newsletter Sign Up

Acknowledgments

To my mom, who made me feel safe straying from the beaten path and who held my hand along the way.

To every English teacher who ever made me feel like my words were worth reading.

To everyone that hurt me or loved me or touched me enough for me to write a poem for you.